AF572303

THE POETESS

Helen Ruggieri

Uroboros Books/Allegany Mountain Press

Poems by the Poetess have appeared in the magazines Primer, Aevum, Images, and as a chapbook published by this press in 1977.

Library of Congress Cataloging in Publication Data

Ruggieri, Helen, 1938-
The poetess.

Includes index.
I. Title.
PS3568.U365P6 811'.5'4 79-18883
ISBN 0-931588-09-X
ISBN 0-931588-10-3 pbk.

FOR THE MOTHERS

her mother's name was Lilith
mine is Lily

CONTENTS

THE POETESS DIGS UP HER DAHLIAS

It's one of the last days to dig up dahlia tubers
before the snow   the platter blossoms are soft
and black   orange chinese lanterns sprawl along
the fence, red berberries spot the mud   yellow
beech leaves, brown apples leaves lie on the rank
grass rusty with larch needles   she works in a
frenzy, forcing the spade into the mud, lifting
the clumps carefully, gently tapping the mud
from the tubers, turning them upside down
emptying water from the hollow stems, setting
them aside on the grass   in her head she's
setting it all down - what she just described
for you   she's making her whole life like that

THE POETESS MEDITATES IN HER GARDEN

behind the garage by the compost pile
she has her meditation garden with
raked gravel swirling away and large
representative stones and sometimes
a gnarled olive tree leaning south
bent by prevailing winds   she sits
on the splintery hemlock bench by
the rotting orange rinds, coffee grounds
egg shells, potato peels, while a cricket
measures off her luck till frost   in her
garden she has whatever she wants

THE POETESS SHAKES HER FIST AT THE EQUINOX

wind throwing leaves at her - beech, apple
oak, maple - north wind blowing the leaves
larch tree throwing brown needles at her
jealous of the pine   giving her the needle
stabbing her in the back   every autumn
losing everything   this betrayal   always
committing herself to summer   always
being left behind

THE POETESS (NOTING THE SIGNS) CONFRONTS THE POSSIBILITIES

she only knows winter is coming   it robs fall of
all the color   how will I get through it, she asks
she thinks of a guru, a high priest of the psyche
who will breathe into her, fan the spark she knows
is there, but she knows they'll only want to modi
her behavior, give her drugs, electric shock, blow
her out like an egg, paint her up, send her home
in an Easter basket

THE POETESS THROWS THE COINS

on the Conrail embankment scrub sumac
hold red spires against a cold fall blue sky
cold and sharp   like an omen   all day
long the image persists: sumac holding
red fingers against the blue   earth
meeting spirit   red against blue
nothing furthers   success

THE POETESS LISTENS TO THE WEATHER REPORT

the prediction says 35 degrees tonight
5 to 10 degrees colder in low lying inland
valleys   she closes the storm windows
the tracks are full of brown needles
she pricks her finger   will I fall into a
deep sleep she asks the window?

THE WINDS

she writes: I walk the red, gold paths the
maples lay that move and rustle and
disappear, blown, rushing down the lawn swept
street   I hold myself against the breath

THE POETESS REPEATS THE SYMPTOMS

before she closes up, freezes up, gives up
she recites it all again: crickets, leaves
rain, needles, cold, frost, snow, arcing
out of Hudson Bay over the Lakes to bury her
forcing blood to the marrow, forcing her to
layer herself against the force   don't
think I don't take it personally, she shouts
my subject is always me

THE POETESS DABBLES IN PROPHECY

she writes: I am the stalk
I represent the withering
I represent the blossoming
I hold within the force
it is pulling my head down
drawing up my knees   the
slow tightening of the knotted cord

THE POETESS GOES DOWN

she was raking the leaves when it hit her
like someone supremely tall had snapped
her legs off   she falls over in the leaves
surrounded by an egg of her own pain
impervious   she does not hear the leaves
crackle under her weight nor smell the dry
dust of their passing   she will not get up
whats the use   what for   why should
she   she'll stay here, perhaps until spring
warm beneath the leaves

THE MYTH OF CURING

there is blight   at the ceremony of curing
a maiden at her first menses runs through
the fields on a moonless night   her power
spent she is split   head to crotch
one half buried at the east   the other
at the west   such savage ceremonies
are the beginning

THE POETESS DOES BATTLE AGAINST THE WINTER

cold   leaking in around the windows
the doorsill where the weather stripping
is worn away   the double windows not
thick enough to keep out artic cold that
circles over the Lake to drive the blood
in closer to the marrow   to hide at the
center   the busy cold that stills and stills

THE POETESS REREADS
EDNA SAINT VINCENT MILLAY

she writes: numbness and sensibility sit
on my head like a bloodcap   there is no
escaping the decision of genes   they have
their own will set in lavender and pale yellow
vibrating like sonnets in the mystical darkness
full prayers of brass and percussion   the
numbness thickens and sensibility says
even Millay is boring and dead

THE PARABLE OF THE VINE

brown sticks of the clematis vine
wind around the trellis   waver in
the wind   the roots mounded with
larch needles against the cold
she writes: I am warm and
comfortable   there is no light

THE POETESS VISITS HER GYNECOLOGIST

bare feet up in cold stirrups submitting to this
metalic rape, this objective view, this naked
interlude   he is unaffected by her vulnerability
looking for whatever he looks for at the end of
the dark tunnel   she thinks if I could project
the inner gift would his face change from doctor
to wonder having seen the light?

THE POETESS REREADS CHRISTINA ROSETTI

she knows all about being alone, healing
herself, being in a place she herself creates
filled with dead poets, tv stars, characters
from novels, dreams, her life is like a reel
of film, video tape, plots, clustered images
frozen in a still photo   she is wrapped in
ribbons of tape, a billion images stretching
around her, illuminated by a pale yellow light
projecting from somewhere behind her right
eye, somewhere deep within her body

THE POETESS WATCHES TOO MUCH TELEVISION

she stares   wrapped in her bright serape
she stares at the snowy screen   surrounded
by her tropical plants she stares out an
alien window at the endless falling snow

THE WINTER WAY

driving to Salamanca she loses the road
in blowing snow   on the right the mountain
on the left the black Allegheny waters
the snow squalls like a sunburst   an
explosion   a firecracker against the
windshield   a wild kaliodescope   a
fascination to be avoided   heavy white
trees lure her to the life that goes by
the side   in deep rooted forests   in
ancient groves lit by burning snow where
the priestess waits to mark her for Her own

ALLEGHENY RIVER ANALOGY

she writes: the Allegheny is dark at the center
edged with a fringe of jagged opaque glass
there is movement only at the center
the Allegheny follows it purpose coldly
over the graves of Cornplanters ancestors
over the dam at Kinzua, through the Western
Gate and on and on and on - the Allegheny
just being about its purpose   being beautiful

THE POETESS STARES INTO
THE EYES OF LUCIFER

she is frozen in the mirror   it does not move
nothing happens   nothing changes   stasis
the clock on the dresser does not move
the same eyes return her stare from the mirror
they are still green   there is no light in them
she waits   surely when the spark comes she
will be blinded   struck blind by the invincible light

SELF PORTRAIT

she knows that her motion is circumscribed by
her own fear, her own ineffectual sadness, her
neurotic self pity, her will to power, her failure
to confront her own evil, her original sin, her
past, her breaking of taboo, her unmodifiable
insistance on her omniscient will   she has
built her own wall, her own high tower, her
own glass cell and she is circling around and
around watching the light reflect, distort,
multiply her to infinity   she concentrates to
keep the image, to hold it   it is her only
clue, her only cure

A CHRISTMAS DREAM

she dreams she is old   her hair is white
she is wearing a white hospital gown she is
so very old, she has so little strength she
is all alone   she is so lonely   she is so weak
she cries for herself   but the old one in the
dream sees the red pointsettia on the night
stand and struggles to reach it   to touch it
and she pulls it out of the pot   spilling dirt
across the white sheets and she plants it
that bright red pointsettia   she plants it
between her legs   in her crotch
she points   she laughs   I'm not
dead yet she cackles   not dead yet

THE POETESS BEGINS TO WEEP FOR NO REASON

she is seated in her favorite chair
her hands folded in her lap   her mind
empty of everything but the picture of
her hands folded in her lap   for no
reason she begins to cry and she resents
it, knows it will allow her to somehow
continue   she rages at the bodys
interference with her will

KEEPING THE MIDWINTER CEREMONY

she reads: the Iroquois believed dreams were
the voice of the great spirit speaking directly
to them   five days past the new January
moon all dreams were interpreted, fulfilled
commemorated   the Jesuits recorded they
were used for cures, a mania they translated
as "turning the brain upsidedown"   she
rereads all those dreams she has written
in her ledger labeled "The Sound of Light"

THE POETESS IS STRUCK BY
THE FORCE OF MEMORY

pulling clothes out of the dryer she feels the hair
on her arms rise, the hair on her head move across
her face   she pulls two orlon sweaters apart and
the crackling sends vibrations through her whole
body   as she reaches for the doorknob a long
jagged yellow spark meets her hand   it hurts
it hurts all the way up to her elbow   she
had forgotten

THE POETESS DREAMS HER HANDS HURT

out of a certain terror that the future will contine
as the endless present, out of a full knowledge
of the persistance of cold which will continue
to extinguish every restless gesture, out there
somewhere through the glass she thinks she
will see a sign   she longs to hammer at the
glass, to break through, but her hands are
curled with arthritis, painful and knotted
and she is powerless, unable to reach for
what she imagines she sees out there

THE POETESS HAS HER PICTURE TAKEN

the snow glazed with ice is too bright
painful in the full sun   her small face
stares unsmiling into the camera   to
her left she casts a huge black shadow
three times her own size it stretches off
into the margins   she thinks she can
make out a smiling face in this black
undulation   she smiles back faintly
nodding her head as she stares at it
noticing the painful image of contrast
so perfectly recorded here before her

IN THE DEAD OF WINTER
THE POETESS DEFIES GRAVITY

she opens a pack of cigarettes
the cellophane wrapper sticks
to her hand   her whole arm
shaking, she raises it parallel
to the floor and turns her palm
down   the cellophane remains
in her open hand

THE POETESS CELEBRATES PUNXSUTAWNEY PHIL

she reads: on the first of February fires were
lit on the highest points, to show the sun the
way back   to call back the sun   to remind her
the groundhog has seen his shadow on that frigid
Pennsylvania hilltop announcing there will be
six more long weeks to study the remnants of
myths containing the cold   she dreams his
thin shrill voice calling the sun back

THE POETESS SEES A SIGN IN THE SNOW

she walks to the store   only cigarettes
could bring her out on a night like this
the wind drives frozen pellets of snow
into her face as she walks west down
state street   in the fresh snow on the
sidewalk she sees the mark of the fish
there are no footprints but hers leading
to this place

THE POETESS READIES FOR BED

she wears heavy sweaters and wraps herself
in her serape to keep warm   she unwraps
for bed pulling a sweater over her head in
the dark a flame cracks around her hair
flying out all edged in yellow   uneasy
she gets into bed, dreams of herself wrapped
in linen, closed in a sarcophagus, her arms
bound at her sides, palms touching her thighs
she feels them   they are still warm
she wakes up   the streetlight shows
her the african violet is in bloom

THE POETESS DESCRIBES THE THAW FROM HER BEDROOM WINDOW

the yard is bright today in February sun
the black garden dirt she turned last fall
is bare, the grass still covered with the
melting remains of drifts - crusted, gray
she sits in the window with the african
violet and feels the sun on her

THE POETESS GIVES THANKS TO THE MAPLE

not far from here she writes the long house
people are celebrating the first festival of
spring   they are giving thanks for the maple
giving thanks for the sweet water that rises
in the maple   life returns to the dead trees
the maple sings: the sweetness of life is
come   the sweetness

THE POETESS SEES HER VISIT TO THE DENTIST AS A PARADIGM

in the chair she thinks of the inner light
rising from her throat to sparkle in the
mirror but she only sighs into the numb-
ness staring at the pasteboard painting
of a blue lake surrounded by pine trees
she hardly notices the dentist with his
instruments   she puts herself under
a pine tree in the picture, plops pebbles
into the water   waits for it to be over

THE POETESS HEARS A VOICE IN THE NIGHT

the man in the turban knocks at her window
knocks at her door, pounds on her door
he is banging, clashing golden cymbols
banging them together, making a terrible
din, a terrible noise   she covers her
ears but can't escape - get up, get up
get up, he chants   all day long the
rhythm follows her - typewriters click
it, radio sings it, car engine mocks it
everywhere, all day long it follows her
repeats   half asleep she becomes aware
of someone whispering it softly over and
over   she recognizes the voice   it is
her own

IN THE HANDS LIES THE FUTURE

as Lent approaches she feels the tension
increasing   she stares at her hands
expecting stigmata   notes the pale
blue tinged nails   marks the curious
absence of white half moons rising
out of the quick   she folds her hands
into fists, squeezes hard   as she
opens them she sees the nails have
made a series of small red parentheses
across the life line

THE CLEANSING VIRTUE

the rage puffs out like a breath
in the cold air, a white cloud
which swells, merges, disappears
absorbed in the invisible barrier
surrounding her   when she is done
has cursed all she knows, only the
weakness is left, the total exhaustion
that follows such consuming rage

POINT OF NO RETURN

the poetess whines a high shrill note
she is so enraged she does not hear it
she is beside herself   split off
she plays out the scene   venting
her anger, revelling in the feel of it
this invincibility, this momentary
power surging through her while
another part of her watches
disinterested, objective - a curious
duplication she thinks, odd

THE POETESS SELECTS HER LENTEN REGIMEN

40 days to think about death   to mourn
our humanity   to impersonate the spiritual
to give up   to deny what we are   to practice
what we would be   her own body hangs on
her like a rag on a tree limb   she wishes
she were pure spirit like the north wind that
slices through frail tissue   she looks at
her hands   they are the hands of a ghost
she once knew   she will eat only red meat
these 40 days   the hunters diet

LENTEN SEQUENCE

SONG OF THE BONES: THE POETESS REREADS 'ASH WEDNESDAY'

she writes: because I do not hope
to pray for the hour   under the hour
the inevitable turning hour   under
the larch tree the bones are scattered
and white   singing the song of wind
and the fierceness of March   cutting
the flesh from living bones   songless
sunken under the ritual earth   silent
and holy

I do not hope to turn the righteous hand
that marks the forehead   the smudge
of ashes   the small gray eye of hope-
lessness   40 days under the gray death
sign   hollow and silent   mother of
bones   salient taste of ashes and gray
silence   the bitter wind hurling bare
larch branches   this cemetery of seed
rosette cones falling to litter the earth

I do not hope to see the earth turning
I pray to see the earth turning   the
dull earth   the same dun color every
where   the raw look of an unfinished
world   every where the same   the
silent bones in their place

only words to hope the wind will sing
over the dead   in the wilderness
the hopeless turning wilderness
thumbprint of death on the brow and
only words to sing the wind of fierce
and silent death   to call the wind its
description   to curse what weighs so
heavy on the dead   unrepenting paradox
unwhole and holy   to come again and
turn and burrow in the plowed earth and
40 days of stillness and wrath

silent bones scraped clean by the wind
will be unearthed, gathered, blood
drenched, wrapped in the still warm
sacrificial hide to live again   to sing
and celebrate the resurrection   the broken
ground   the ground broken   the earth
broken into its receptive pose

perhaps there is a turning in the dark
there is a movement   a voice
a warming wind   some voiceless
promise prodded and jabbed   perhaps
a worm has brushed against them in
their sleep   beginning the curious
turning   the turning that begins
this gray day   this grayest day

THE POETESS MEDITATES ON MAUNDY THURSDAY

she has gotten into bed to meditate
she settles into her night place with
dream remnants, fantasies, old
nightmares   she smells her own
peculiar scent   old perfume
released by her warmth   she stares
out the window determined to stay
awake, to meditate   she watches
the pine limbs rise and fall in the wind
staring into the complex of pine edged
by the window frame she sees a face
bare branches delineate the forehead
the mouth is hidden by a claw, a
knotted gnarled hand   she stares
at it moving in and out of focus in
the wind   from her night place she
sees her face even in the trees   like
this it is an extension of her need

GOOD FRIDAY MEDITATIO

she sees herself again in the pine tree
her face hidden in the crossing branches
her body   she is hanging   no, she is nailed
nailed to the tree   she is stretched and taut
like an animal skin   a pelt a parchment
fine vellum   she feels the surface   smooth
for writing and indestructible   she sees words
on it   strains to read   to focus   yes, this
is it   she must see   the indestructible word
as she watches the tree grows, encircles the
parchment   absorbs it into itself   the words
come to her   this is the tree of the knowledge
of good and evil   this is the tree of time
this is the universe that goes on without her
this is the turning   now   it says   now
she begins a poem entitled: The Knowledge
of the Tree is Death

THE KNOWLEDGE OF THE TREE IS DEATH

this then is crucifixion   this is cleaving
the apple   getting at the core   dividing
cutting through   separating   this is the
heart of it   the apple sliced in half
this is the fruit of the tree and the black
tear shaped seeds are the eternal feminine
this is the labor   this is the birth
this is the light   this is the death
here is the apple   take it and eat

HOLY SATURDAY: A DAY OF WAITING

there is an unexpected snowfall during the night
huge light drifts of spring snow cover the small
saffron and purple crocus blossoms   the yard
is hushed, silent, mounded by the winds care-
less sweep   it is a day of fasting, of abstinance
a day of waiting   even this will not stop the
future   she runs out barefoot in the snow
makes her own imprint   her own fallen
angel in the unmarked snow

EASTER SUNDAY: EPIPHANY

she is in the yard studying the red spears
of emerging peony   suddenly she is
impapled on the red spears   tied to the
earth   they have pierced her through
there is no blood   there is no pain
she relaxes into the receptive mud
the rich brown mud   curitive powers
of the earth draw the evil from her,
the sickness   they flow from her into
the earth and she is consumed in the raging
blue flames almost invisible against the
cold blue sky while tears shaped like blue
flames fall from her eyes   tears for what
is lost   the nature of time   of purpose
she rises from her old body and assumes
the lotus   from her upraised right hand
a white flower grows shaped like a bowl
and she knows that in her left, held
down and closed there is a small blue
tear shaped like a flame
she remains there for a long time

PRAYING THE RAIN

rain creates the condition of things
praying the silver beaded rosary of rain
praying rain for forgiveness   for the
growth snapping around her above the
heavy mud   who would ask the green
stalk to repent   it comes without my
sins, sacrifices, ceremonies or because
of them   the ground dissolving under
my knees   softening, losing the hardness
my act of contrition mother, forgive me
I know the spring will come with or
without my hubris in calling it down

TWO DAYS COME TOGETHER IN HER MIND

WINTER SOLSTICE

wet heavy snow clings to bare branched maples
lining the street   creating black and white
complexities against the low pearl clouds
sometime late this afternoon the earth
will pass an invisible line out in space
the sun will appear to stand still, to stop
the quality of light will diminish   it will
be colder   snow will pile on pine branches
reaching like awkward paws to hold us in a
merciless grasp   change is a long way off
we will appear to stand still against the light

VERNAL EQUINOX

streaks of melting snow undulate down the hill
gleaming in the gray light   soon it will rain
and this evening   sometime after 6 p.m. we
will spin past an invisible line out in space
slowly light will begin its lengthening triumph
as we turn to face the sun   this slow turning
hear the water overflowing the eaves   the
lusty smell rising from the thawing soil
a few hours more   a few hours more

THE CONJUNCTION

these two days come together in her mind
these two days colored the same gray
their exact shade drawn by her lifetime
by evolution, foreknowledge, hindsight
they come together   invisible lines
plotting the galaxy   careful scientific
observation   mythic moments   ancient
knowledge   she reads: in ancient
planting societies a priest dressed in
the flayed skin of a sacrificed maiden
walks through the barren fields chanting
in his ritual footsteps will rise the corn

THE POETESS DREAMS HER RIGHT HAND

as the first full moon follows the vernal equinox
the poetess dreams she marks the doorway
with menstrual blood against the angel of death
she hears the singers celebrating Kore's return
to her mother carrying the newborn child
pigs are sacrificed   honey cakes sprinkled
with blood are tossed to copulating snakes
she is pushed forward   a staff is in her
right hand

THE POETESS BEGINS A POEM AT WORK

telephones ring, typewriters electrically repeat
voices explore, question, ease in even tones
out the window a spring yellow willow is
illuminated by a ray of sun from between the
low gray clouds heavy with threat   she
watches this radiant island until the clouds
close off the light   she jots it down on her
memo pad: willow   yellow   gray
she folds the paper in half, rips it back and
forth, lets it cascade like snowflakes into
the basket   willow, yellow, gray
willow, yellow, gray   she likes the sound

ANALOGY OF THE FORSYTHIA

there is a fine penetrating drizzle
as she struggles to capture all the
nuance of terrain and color she is
stopped short by the fact that only
the forsythia seems worthy of
attention - an incredible yellow
in the misty air   she writes:
only the brightest yellow attracts the
mind feeding on itself in the pregnant air

THE POETESS WALKS THE YARD

the sun is out   its the first warm day
she tours the yard noticing daffodil
spears pointed up almost two inches
above the mud   they seem to grow
while she watches   she pulls away
the wet black leaves to ease their
progress

THE POETESS REMEMBERS JANUARY

the poetess thinks back to January   she
remembers wondering how the pioneers survived
how the Eskimos survive   why they want to
she remembers thinking she would die in January
caught in the middle she would give up   never
come back   she looks at the bed of daffodils
she will try to hold it in her mind   this clear
yellow light   the pure lucid scent they trumpet
into the world   how they spark against the
black wet earth

THE POETESS COMPARES THE NATURE OF WEEDS

she begins to weed the flower bed, to pull
the rank field grass that grows in the wrong
place, pulling dandelions from between
forget-me-nots and dog toothed violets
crowding the red tulips   she thinks about
the growth of what she cultivates and what
grows without her care   eating at the border
the neat edge she'd lined lost in the green
struggle

THE POETESS HAS HER HAIR CUT

it falls to the spackled linoleum
dark wet snakey strands   shorn
medusa   shorn medusa
she does not ignore omens
in the mirror she appears to be
someone else   her face is an
image within an image stretching
back as far as there is   she traces
the shining faces as far as she can
somethings never change nor should
they

THE POETESS PUTS IN HER DAHLIAS

she is planting dahlia tubers when her eye
catches something in a pile of upturned earth
she picks it up, spits on it, wipes it on her
shirt   its a wedding ring   inside there are
no initials, just the legend "solid gold"
she places in on her right index finger, her
Jupiter finger, finger of will, of direction
its a perfect fit   its hers   she may have
lost it in another life, she has, in fact,
been searching for it a long time   she
holds her hand out, admires the way the
sun sparkles on the gold   she marvels at
the way everything comes together   she
begins to laugh, she laughs so hard she cries